At Last

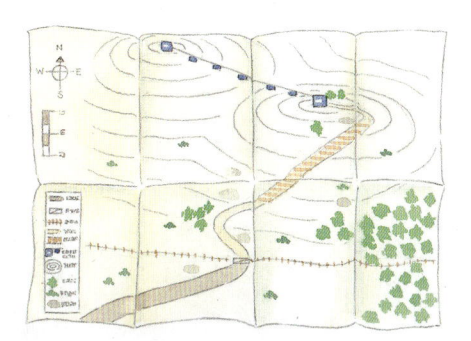

Alison Hawes
Illustrated by Sami Sweeten

We went out for a walk.
We went up the road.

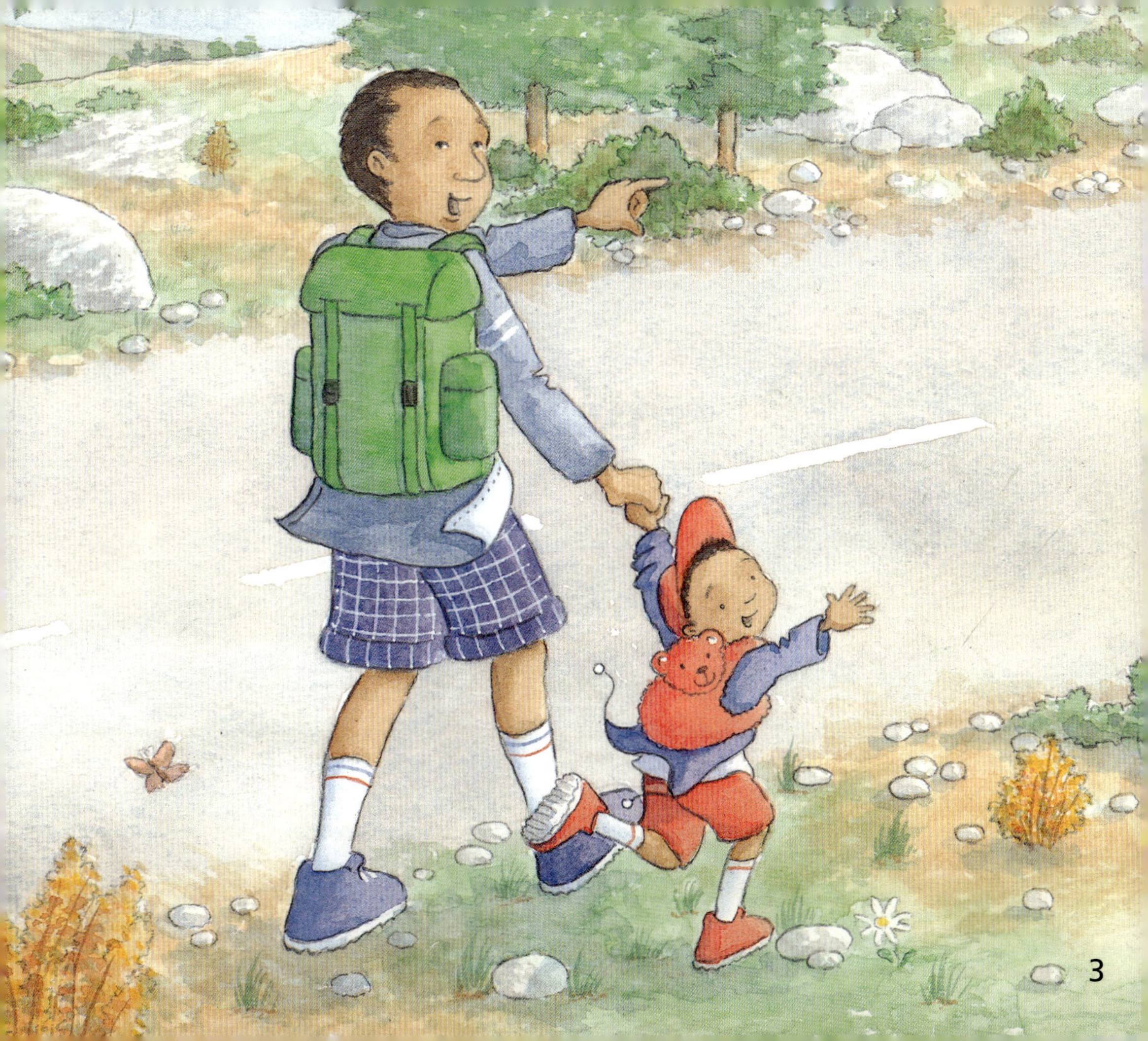

At the end of the road . . .

Path

we came to a path.
We went up the path.

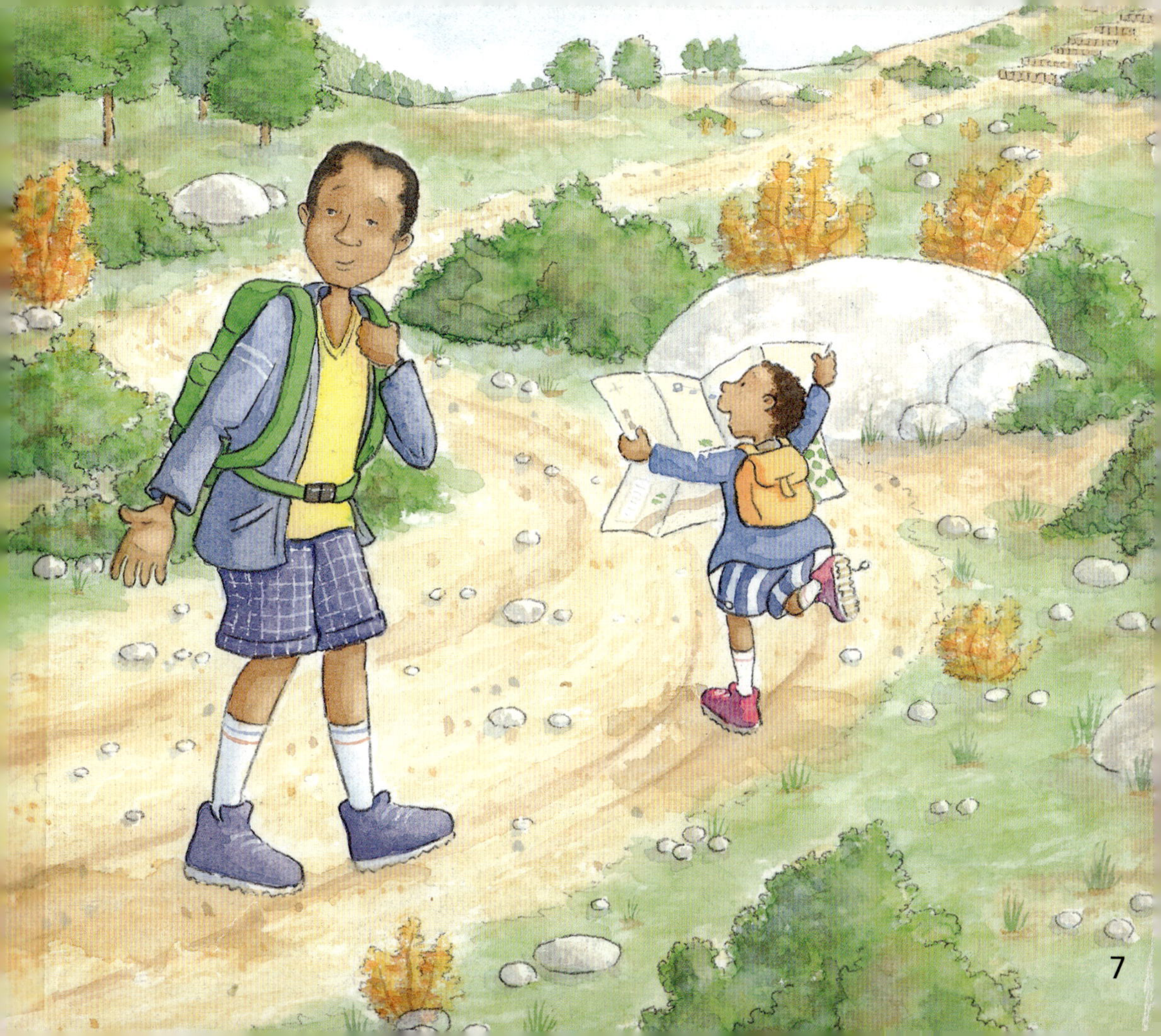

At the end of the path . . .

9

we came to some steps.
We went up the steps.

11

At the end of the steps...

Lift

we came to a lift.
We went up in the lift.

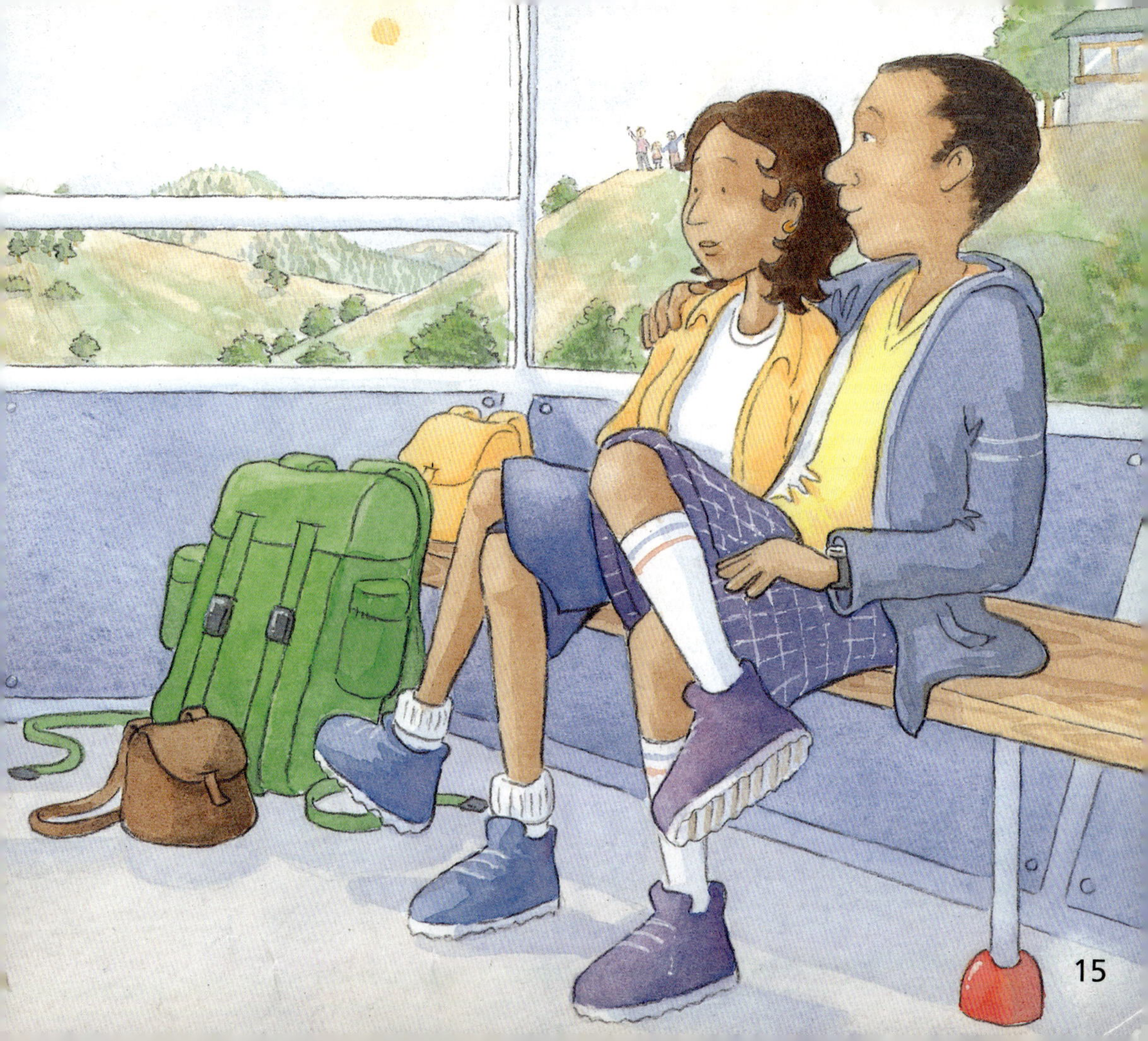

At last! We had our picnic!